It Starts With a Bee

Inspiring | Educating | Creating | Entertaining

Brimming with creative inspiration, how-to
projects, and useful information to enrich your
everyday life, quarto.com is a favorite destination
for those pursuing their interests and passions.

Words by Aimee Gallagher
Illustrations by Jennie Webber

Editor: Nancy Dickmann
Editorial Assistant: Alice Hobbs
Art Director: Susi Martin
Publisher: Holly Willsher

First published in 2022 by QED Publishing,
an imprint of The Quarto Group
The Old Brewery, 6 Blundell Street,
London, N7 9BH United Kingdom.
T (0)20 7700 6700 F (0)20 7700 8066
www.quarto.com

A catalogue record for this book is available from the British Library.

ISBN: 978-0-7112-7033-6

9 8 7 6 5 4 3 2 1

Manufactured in Guangdong, China CC012022

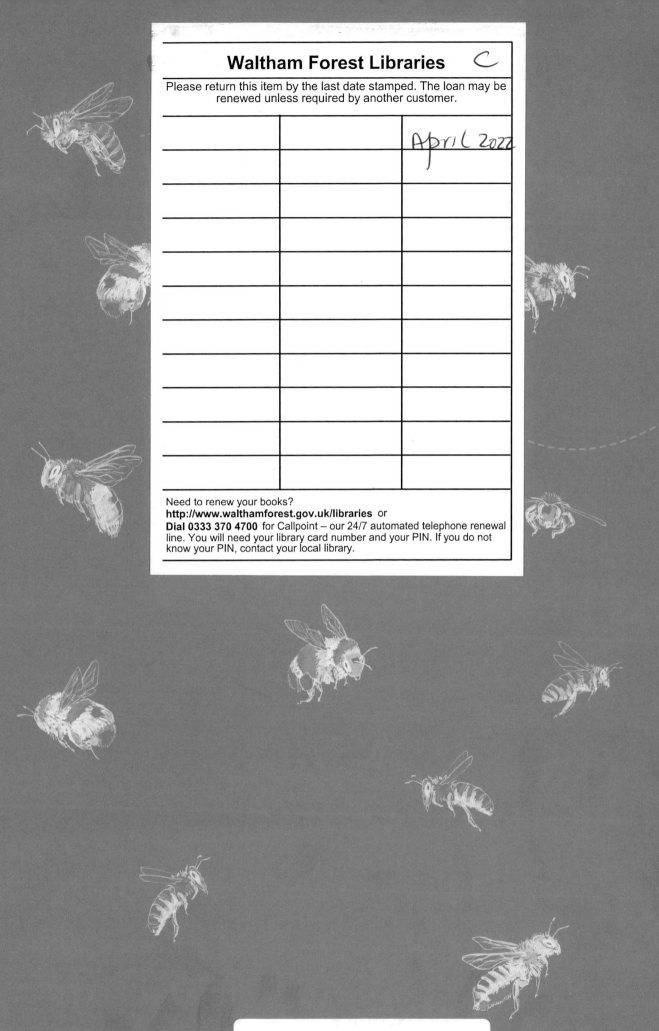

It Starts With a Bee

Pictures by Jennie Webber

It starts with a bee...

But where does it lead?

In winter they huddle,
all eyes facing in.
When the temperature rises,
their work can begin!

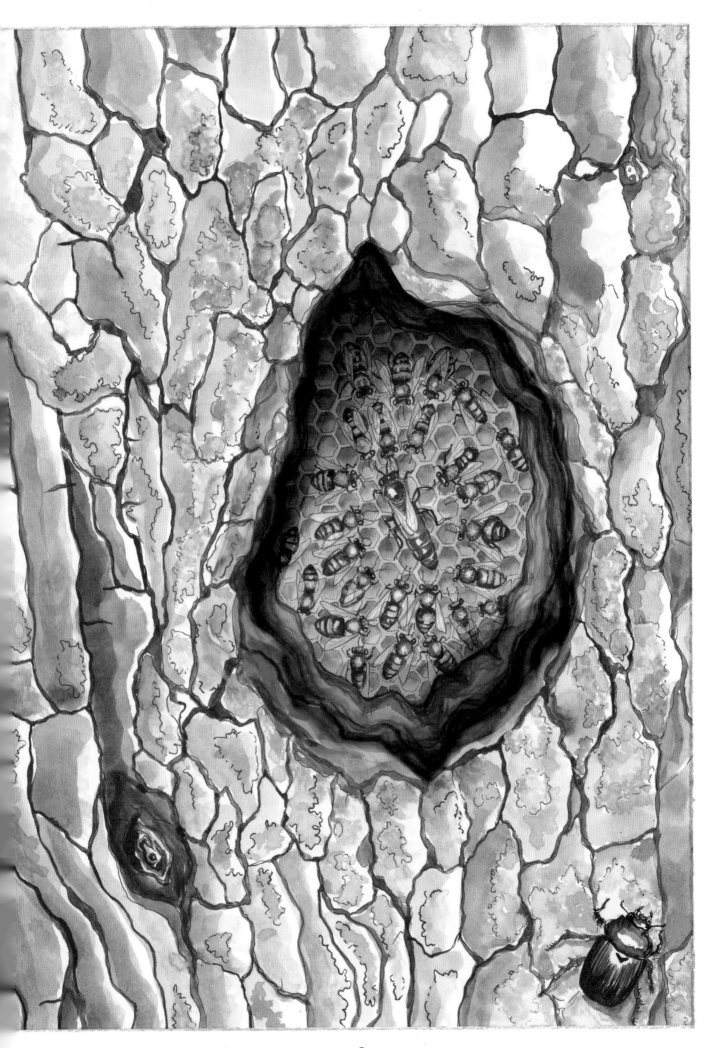

The food stores are empty,
spring calls them outside;
what sweet scents and bright colours
in vistas so wide!

Snowdrops, daffodils,

crocus and daisy:

they flock to these beacons,

no time to be lazy!

Sweet nectar lures them.

They nose into each bloom,

drinking sugary goodness, then

again, off they zoom!

They fill up their saddlebags
bulging and pollen-y,

then buzz swiftly back to dispatch
to their colony.

They wiggle and waggle,

to show to their friends

just where to find flowers

on which to descend.

Then it's back to the garden
to find more to eat,
with pollen now stuck to their legs,
sides and feet.

The pollen rubs off
as they dart to and fro,
and inside each flower
a fruit starts to grow.

As spring turns to summer,
more petals unfurl.

The garden's a larder through
which the bees whirl.

The plants form a haven where
creatures are found,
from insects on green leaves to
worms underground.

Bees tirelessly fly through
this minibeast town,
their gentle buzz humming as the
sun settles down.

Thanks to diligent bees...

...working hard in a bunch...

Stigma   Ovule

As the bee collects nectar from the next flower, some pollen will rub off from her hairs onto the plant's female part, the stigma.

The pollen fertilises this flower's egg cells, or ovules. After fertilisation, the female parts of the flower develop into fruit containing seeds.

Without pollinators like bees, flowers could not produce fruit or distribute seeds so that new plants can grow.

The process of pollination

The beautiful flowers in this book attract bees through their scent, brightly coloured petals and shape.

Nectar is found in the nectaries at the base of a flower's petals. When the bee collects the sweet nectar, pollen from the plant's male part, the stamen, rubs off onto her hairy legs and body.

This bee will then visit another flower to collect more nectar.

A bee can visit up to 100 flowers per flight.

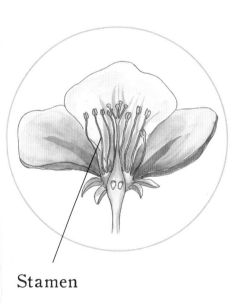

Stamen

...fruits swell and ripen...

...to end up in our lunch!

Different types of bees

There are more than 20,000 known species of bee. They don't all produce honey, or nest in large groups of other bees, but they all have important roles.

Bumblebees have plump, fuzzy bodies and are usually larger than honeybees. They have a very important job pollinating flowers and crops. They live in colonies of up to 200 bees and often nest in holes in the ground or under garden sheds, piles of wood or leaves.

Honeybees are usually smaller and thinner than bumblebees. They live in very large hives of thousands of bees and produce honey. Some live in man-made beehives, while others build hives in hollow trees or crevices, using the beeswax that they produce.

Carpenter Bees look like bumblebees with hairless, shiny black abdomens. They live alone rather than in large groups and pollinate flowers and plants. They nest by tunnelling into wood where they lay their eggs.

Digger Bees can be large or small, hairy or shiny, but they all have an important role as pollinators. They nest alone in underground burrows, near other digger bees.

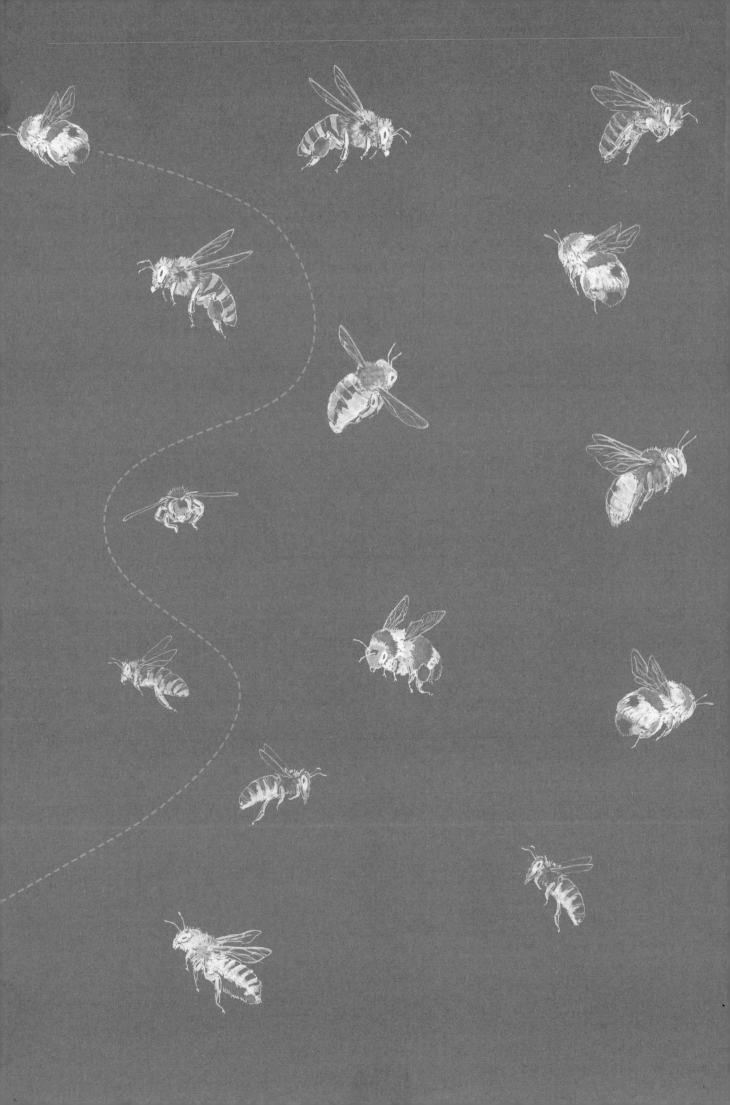